STEPHANIE STREET

Stephanie Street is an actor, writer and director, born and raised in Singapore. She read English at Jesus College, Cambridge, before training as an actor on a scholarship at LAMDA.

Plays include an adaptation of *The Reluctant Fundamentalist*, shortlisted for Amnesty International's Freedom of Expression Award and the Carol Tambor Best of Edinburgh Award (Finborough Theatre/The Yard/Summerhall, Edinburgh); *Force Majeure*, an adaptation of Chekhov's *Three Sisters*; and *Dragonflies,* Straits Times Life Theatre Awards for Best Original Script and Production of the Year (Victoria Theatre, Singapore). Her first play, *Sisters*, re-opened the Sheffield Crucible Studio after the theatre's refurbishment in 2010.

As an actor, theatre credits include *Coriolanus*, *Behind the Beautiful Forevers*, *King James Bible: The Gospel According to John* and *Nightwatchman*, WhatsOnStage Award nomination – Best Solo Performance (National Theatre); *The Inquiry*, *Our Generation* (Minerva/National Theatre); *Quiz* (Minerva/West End/Chichester Festival Theatre); *Shades* (Royal Court). Recent TV work includes *A Good Girl's Guide to Murder season 2*, *The Lady*, *Joan* and *Breathtaking*.

Stephanie co-founded Act for Change, campaigning for representative diversity in the industry and is diversity champion on the board of Chichester Festival Theatre.

Other Titles in this Series

Waleed Akhtar
THE ART OF ILLUSION *after* Alexis Michalik
KABUL GOES POP: MUSIC TELEVISION AFGHANISTAN
THE P WORD
THE REAL ONES

Chris Bush
THE ASSASSINATION OF KATIE HOPKINS *with* Matt Winkworth
THE CHANGING ROOM
CHRIS BUSH PLAYS: ONE
A DOLL'S HOUSE *after* Ibsen
FAUSTUS: THAT DAMNED WOMAN
HUNGRY
JANE EYRE *after* Brontë
THE LAST NOËL
OTHERLAND
ROBIN HOOD AND THE CHRISTMAS HEIST *with* Matt Winkworth
ROCK / PAPER / SCISSORS
STANDING AT THE SKY'S EDGE *with* Richard Hawley
STEEL

Jez Butterworth
THE FERRYMAN
THE HILLS OF CALIFORNIA
JERUSALEM
JEZ BUTTERWORTH PLAYS: ONE
JEZ BUTTERWORTH PLAYS: TWO
MOJO
THE NIGHT HERON
PARLOUR SONG
THE RIVER
THE WINTERLING

Alexi Kaye Campbell
ALEXI KAYE CAMPBELL PLAYS: ONE
APOLOGIA
BIRD GROVE
BRACKEN MOOR
THE FAITH MACHINE
THE PRIDE
SUNSET AT THE VILLA THALIA

Caryl Churchill
BLUE HEART
CHURCHILL PLAYS: THREE
CHURCHILL PLAYS: FOUR
CHURCHILL PLAYS: FIVE
CHURCHILL: SHORTS
CLOUD NINE
DING DONG THE WICKED
A DREAM PLAY *after* Strindberg
DRUNK ENOUGH TO SAY I LOVE YOU?
ESCAPED ALONE
FAR AWAY
GLASS. KILL. BLUEBEARD'S FRIENDS. IMP.
HERE WE GO
HOTEL
ICECREAM
LIGHT SHINING IN BUCKINGHAMSHIRE
LOVE AND INFORMATION
MAD FOREST
A NUMBER
PIGS AND DOGS
SEVEN JEWISH CHILDREN
THE SKRIKER
THIS IS A CHAIR
THYESTES *after* Seneca
TRAPS
WHAT IF IF ONLY

David Haig
THE GOOD SAMARITAN
MAGIC
MY BOY JACK
PRESSURE

Dave Harris
TAMBO & BONES
TENDER

Lucy Kirkwood
BEAUTY AND THE BEAST *with* Katie Mitchell
BLOODY WIMMIN
THE CHILDREN
CHIMERICA
HEDDA *after* Ibsen
THE HUMAN BODY
IT FELT EMPTY WHEN THE HEART WENT AT FIRST BUT IT IS ALRIGHT NOW
LUCY KIRKWOOD PLAYS: ONE
MOSQUITOES
NSFW
RAPTURE
TINDERBOX
THE WELKIN

Katherine Moar
FARM HALL
RAGDOLL

Ava Pickett
1536
BLOODSPORT: AFTER HELEN OF TROY
EMMA *after* Austen
THE MANNINGTREE WITCHES *after* A. K. Blakemore

Winsome Pinnock
THE AUTHENTICATOR
LEAVE TAKING
PIG HEART BOY *after* Malorie Blackman
ROCKETS AND BLUE LIGHTS
TAKEN
TITUBA

Tracey Scott Wilson
THE STORY

Jack Thorne
2ND MAY 1997
AFTER LIFE *after* Hirokazu Kore-eda
BUNNY
BURYING YOUR BROTHER IN THE PAVEMENT
A CHRISTMAS CAROL *after* Dickens
THE END OF HISTORY…
HOPE
JACK THORNE PLAYS: ONE
JACK THORNE PLAYS: TWO
JUNKYARD
LET THE RIGHT ONE IN *after* John Ajvide Lindqvist
THE MOTIVE AND THE CUE
MYDIDAE
THE SOLID LIFE OF SUGAR WATER
STACY & FANNY AND FAGGOT
WHEN YOU CURE ME
WHEN WINSTON WENT TO WAR WITH THE WIRELESS
WOYZECK *after* Büchner

debbie tucker green
BORN BAD
DEBBIE TUCKER GREEN PLAYS: ONE
DIRTY BUTTERFLY
EAR FOR EYE
HANG
NUT
A PROFOUNDLY AFFECTIONATE, PASSIONATE DEVOTION TO SOMEONE (– NOUN)
RANDOM
STONING MARY
TRADE & GENERATIONS
TRUTH AND RECONCILIATION

Stephanie Street

a small and quiet light

NICK HERN BOOKS
London
www.nickhernbooks.co.uk

A Nick Hern Book

a small and quiet light first published in Great Britain in 2026 as a paperback original by Nick Hern Books Limited, The Glasshouse, 49a Goldhawk Road, London W12 8QP

Front cover image by Bob King Creative for Chichester Festival Theatre; photograph of Priyanga Burford as Noor by Seamus Ryan
Back cover image of Noor-un-Nisa Inayat Khan courtesy of The National Archives (Catalogue Reference: HS9-836-5)

Designed and typeset by Nick Hern Books, London
Printed in the UK by Mimeo Ltd, Huntingdon, Cambridgeshire PE29 6XX

A CIP catalogue record for this book is available from the British Library

ISBN 978 1 83904 587 5

Woodland CARBON
www.woodlandcarbon.co.uk
NICK HERN BOOKS
Printed on Carbon Captured paper

www.nickhernbooks.co.uk/environmental-policy

Nick Hern Books' authorised representative in the EU is
Easy Access System Europe – Mustamäe tee 50, 10621 Tallinn, Estonia
email gpsr.requests@easproject.com

a small and quiet light was first performed at the Minerva Theatre, Chichester, on 21 August 2026, before transferring to the Orange Tree Theatre, Richmond, on 21 September 2026. The cast was as follows:

NOOR-UN-NISA INAYAT KHAN	Priyanga Burford
VOGT	Caoilfhionn Dunne
YOUNG NOOR/PIANIST	Kiah Arya
ABBA/JEPSON/ELISABETH	Paksie Vernon
MAMS/YOLANDE/VIENNOT	Léa des Garets
BHAI/CARTAUD	Tripti Tripuraneni
AMMA/WESSELOW/VERA/KIEFFER	Amanda Hadingue

All other roles played by members of the company

Director	Elin Schofield
Production Dramaturg	Diyan Zora
Designer	Anna Yates
Lighting Designer	Ryan Joseph Stafford
Composer	Nicola T. Chang
Sound Designer	Tingying Dong
Movement Director	Adi Gortler
Fight Director	Sam Lyon-Behan
Casting Director	Jacob Sparrow
Assistant Director	Amy Crighton
Voice and Dialect Coach	Zoe Littleton
Production Manager	Jacqui Leigh
Costume Supervisor	Evelien Van Camp
Props Supervisor	Katie Balmforth
Company Stage Manager	Cheryl Firth
Deputy Stage Manager	Emily Davies
Assistant Stage Manager	Meg Le Marchant

Acknowledgements

I owe profound thanks to the following people:

Prasanna Puwanarajah; Priyanga Burford; Daniel Evans; Kate Bassett; Antoinette Marti; Jean-Marie Maroille; la Société d'Histoire de Suresnes; Justin Audibert; Kathy Bourne; Hannah Joss; the CFT Playwrights Fund; Tom Littler; William Gregory; the actors who workshopped this across its development – Félicité du Jeu, Sarita Gabony, Anushka Chakravarti, Jay Villiers, Nicholas Khan, Marc Elliott, Mariam Haque, Selma Alkaff and Anna Burnett; Diyan Zora; Elin Schofield; Nicky Wingfield; Dan Usztan; Julien, Asha and Sachin Sylvestre.

S.S.

For Pops

‘All the stars have fallen to the earth. Tomorrow morning I will have to wake up very early to gather them up before the street cleaner comes along’

Noor-un-Nisa Inayat Khan

Characters

NOOR, *Noor-un-Nisa Inayat Khan, also known as Babuli, Nora, Jeanne-Marie, Madeleine and Rolande. From eight to thirty years old*
VOGT, *Ernest Vogt, SD (Sicherheitsdienst) interrogator*
ABBA, *Noor's father, Hazrat Inayat Khan*
BHAI, *Noor's younger brother, Vilayat*
MAMS, *Noor's younger sister, Claire*
AMMA, *Noor's mother, Ameena Begum, also known as Ora Baker*
JEPSON, *Selwyn Jepson, recruiter for the SOE (Special Operations Executive), F Section and writer*
YOLANDE, *Yolande Beekman, wireless operator for SOE, F Section*
WESSELOW, *Major Roger de Wesselow, head of Wanborough Manor training centre*
VERA, *Vera Atkins, Deputy Director, SOE, F Section*
VIENNOT, *Pierre Viennot, French résistant and SFR engineer*
CARTAUD, *Pierre Cartaud, Frenchman working for the Gestapo*
KIEFFER, *Josef Kieffer, commander of the SD, Paris*
And SOE RECRUITS, GESTAPO GUARDS *in France and Germany*

Note on Play

a small and quiet light is a fictional imagination based on the real events of the life of Noor-un-Nisa Inayat Khan between 1914–1944, as documented through archive records, war records and numerous autobiographies.

Note on Performance

The characters speak in many different languages to each other – English, French, German – but we predominantly only receive it in English. Moments of other languages denote where they have switched into a language for a discrete moment of action or thought.

There is some specified music in the play but it would be ideal if music is everywhere, as it was for Noor.

Note on Text

A forward slash (/) indicates when the next line starts.

This text went to press before the end of rehearsals and so may differ slightly from the play as performed.

ACT ONE

1. Nora Baker Part 1

Paris, 13 October 1943. NOOR *sits opposite* VOGT *in his office in 84 avenue Foch. Her wireless set and notebook are on his desk.*

NOOR. You do. You know who I am!

He stares at her. Inscrutable.

VOGT. I'm afraid I don't.

I know your code name, Madeleine. But of course that's not your real name, is it?

NOOR. You know who I am. What I've done.

A quick glance to her set.

I have nothing to tell you.

VOGT. Right.

He stands.

NOOR. Just one thing in fact. Have me shot. As quickly as possible.

VOGT. Really?

NOOR. Yes.

VOGT. Do you really want that?

NOOR. Most Germans have no fear of guns. Or using them.

VOGT. Most women don't ask to be shot.

NOOR. I'm not like most women.

VOGT. Is that so?

He stands close over her.

NOOR. Try as you like, I will tell you nothing. I'm not afraid of your violence.

That filthy traitor in my apartment – ask him how he enjoyed our fight.

VOGT. You bit a chunk out of his finger.

NOOR. I tasted his blood.

A tiny beat.

VOGT. You didn't want to be caught, did you?

Why not? Who are you protecting?

NOOR. Do you even have a gun?

VOGT. I'm not like most Germans.

NOOR. You look like a German.

VOGT. And you… look like you're hungry. When did you last have a proper meal?

He brings a tray to the table. He pours a cup of tea, milk first, places a few biscuits on the saucer.

The proper English way.

Places the cup in front of her. She pushes it back to him.

He pours himself a cup and replaces hers in front of her. She pushes it back towards him again.

He takes out a packet of cigarettes and lights himself one. She clocks this.

Oh, I'm sorry, do you…?

A faint nod. He holds the packet towards her.

Will you give me what I want in return?

She reaches to take one. He pulls the packet away.

Will you?

NOOR. We'll see, won't we?

He holds the packet out again, she takes one, he lights it for her. He watches her enjoy the first few drags on the cigarette.

VOGT. You're right, there there are… *some* things I know. Code name Madeleine; the name on your papers – Jeanne-Marie. Your cover name, Rolande.

I know that we've been looking for you a long time.

A tiny flicker of pride.

NOOR. Three months.

VOGT. Quite right.

And we had intelligence. Your lovely blue outfit, the strange habit of always carrying your set everywhere you go.

Another glance at her set.

Yet still you… slipped, invisible, through the streets of this beautiful city. Definitely an achievement.

Nothing. NOOR*'s fingers trace her lips between draws on the cigarette.*

I see how resolute you are but, see… you've already given us so much.

Rich information in this notebook of yours.

He flicks through her notebook – she buries her shame.

And your letters…

He takes out a photographed letter.

Help me understand… and I promise to keep you safe.

NOOR. Do you think I believe a word of your promises?

Looking closely at the photograph.

VOGT. …Is this your family name? Baker?

She can't stop herself from reaching out to grab it. He lets her.

NOOR. How did you get this?

VOGT. Ah…

You miss her very much.

NOOR. You… intercept our mail?

VOGT. You don't think you're the only ones who go undercover, do you?

Now, if you talk… tell me who you worked with, what you did, who you really are… then, maybe, you'll see your dear mother again.

Perhaps for her next birthday.

(*Reading.*)…A big kiss and love always and always, Babuli.

So that's you?

2. Babuli 13

Suresnes, August 1926. NOOR*'s* ABBA *sits cross-legged in the Oriental Room at Fazal Manzil.* NOOR, *aged thirteen, sits opposite him.*

ABBA. Man yaerif nafsah yaerif rabah.

NOOR. …I can't.

ABBA. Man yaerif nafsah yaerif rabah –

It's taking a lot for her to try and stay focused.

So what does it mean?

NOOR. Um… He… or I suppose She…

ABBA. It isn't She… But it applies to all humankind, yes. Then?

NOOR. …I don't know, I think it could maybe mean / that –

ABBA. Shh… Stop. Be quiet and listen inwards.

He watches her in silence. She shakes her head. After a moment he relents.

He… or she, who knows himself, knows Allah subhanahu wa ta'ala.

NOOR. Yes.

ABBA. We must be absolutely truthful in the knowledge of ourselves. Mustn't we?

NOOR. Yes, Abba.

ABBA. So we can always live in the white light of God.

We each receive the light in different colours – as if split through a prism – that's what happens in the diverse hearts of men –

She goes to interject.

– yes, or girls… But the source is pure white light. Of truth… Your strong, unchangeable centre.

Because everything's in one – (*He places his hand over her heart.*) and one is in everything. Isn't it?

She nods. Her legs are aching.

So what's in the box I asked you to fetch?

NOOR. This one?

ABBA. That one.

NOOR. Chocolates.

ABBA. Chocolates you've been taking and hiding in your room.

NOOR. Yes.

ABBA. Are they for you?

NOOR. No.

ABBA. You love chocolates.

NOOR. I do. But those aren't for me. They're for the Russians.

ABBA. The Russians.

NOOR. Yes.

He opens the box and pulls out empty foil wrappers.

ABBA. And what are these?

NOOR. Oh, those ones… I ate those.

ABBA. Only… some of them were for the Russians?

NOOR. Mmm-hmm… I didn't think they'd like those ones.

ABBA. No?

NOOR. The colours of the wrappers weren't so nice.

ABBA. I see.

NOOR. But these pretty ones – I heard you and Amma talking about the starvation in Russia, how the children have nothing to eat so I thought… Once I've got enough together, and there's quite a few there now, so, yes, maybe you can send them over now? To the Russian children? What do you think?

She hands the box over to him.

ABBA. I think it's a good idea. As / long…

NOOR. I'm sorry, Abba –

ABBA. Don't be sorry. So long… as you always remember the truthful white light.

NOOR. I will. I promise.

He folds her into a hug. A long moment as they stay like that.

You're not angry?

ABBA. Are you scared of anger?

NOOR. … A little.

ABBA. Well, I'm not. Angry.

A moment.

NOOR. I'm also scared of you leaving. Promise me you won't leave.

ABBA. I felt the same. About my amma. Your daadi.

So when I finally had to leave home, to travel with my father to Nepal – I wasn't much older than / you –

NOOR. How old?

ABBA. Fifteen, I think.

NOOR. Two years older.

ABBA. But I'd never been away from my amma and…

She gave me a little Ganesh statue, pressed it into my breast pocket and she told me, 'He's agreed to be my envoy, to watch over you.' I cried so many nights on that trip.

She strokes his frown lines.

NOOR. Poor you.

ABBA. But the most incredible thing happened. Going up the foothills one day, I slipped and injured my knee –

NOOR. Where?

ABBA. It's fine / now.

NOOR. I want to see.

ABBA *rolls up his left pyjama leg and shows her.*

You can still see the scar.

ABBA. Well, that night… the ache for my amma was greater than it had ever been. I clenched her Ganesha tight in my fist as I slept. And in my dream… she came!

NOOR. No!

ABBA. She did. And she washed my leg and stroked the bridge of my nose and said to me, 'Not long, my beloved son, until we're together.'

When I arrived back to Baroda, months later – before I could say a word, she asked to see my left knee. Because… on that very same day that I'd fallen and had my dream, she also had a dream… that she came to me and washed my leg / and…

NOOR. NO!!

ABBA. Yes. Everything's in one and one is in everything.

A beat.

NOOR. Now you have to tell me the truth – are you leaving?

ABBA. First play me something.

NOOR. Abba!

ABBA. Play what you were practising yesterday.

NOOR. My hands, they keep getting stuck in the same place, / I don't know –

ABBA. Let's listen first, think afterwards.

NOOR *sits at the piano. Plays the opening bars of 'Clair de Lune'.*

Ah… Monsieur Debussy.

NOOR. What was he like?

ABBA. He was small.

NOOR. As small as me?

ABBA. A bit bigger. And his head was solid – like a table. But his hands, when he sat at the piano, they could fly.

She yawns.

Are you too tired?

NOOR. I'm not tired!

ABBA. You went on one of your night-time walks last / night.

NOOR. No!

ABBA. I carried you back to bed.

NOOR. I'm sorry!

ABBA. It's my love's service – no fame or name, my guru would say.

And mine is to carry you.

NOOR. Always?

A tiny moment.

ABBA. I must leave for India in three days, my Bab/uli –

NOOR. Three?!

ABBA. – it's time for me to go home.

NOOR (*a cry from her soul*). No, Abba, please, / please don't –

He places a hand over her heart again.

ABBA. I'll always be here. That indestructible truth, strong as an elephant.

NOOR. But you need to stay with us!

ABBA. No, my Babu.

NOOR. Yes! You do!

She pushes his hand away. He holds a finger to her lips.

ABBA. Shhhh… Shhhhh, listen…

He holds her but it is not a gentle embrace; it is strong, containing.

Say nothing and listen… What do you hear?

There is only the sound of her trying to contain her sobbing. He holds her.

3. Nora Baker Part 2

Paris, 13 October 1943. NOOR *still sitting in* VOGT*'s office, 84 avenue Foch. As he pours more tea he spots her hands fidgeting, playing imaginary piano.*

VOGT. Are you alright?

NOOR. I'll have another cigarette if you've got one.

VOGT. Of course I have one.

But are you going to keep your side of the bargain? And talk?

He takes one for each of them and goes to light hers, but she takes the lighter from him and lights hers herself.

NOOR. I don't know who you are. Why should I tell you who I am?

VOGT. Good point. I'm Vogt. But you can call me Ernest. And what I do here, I translate.

NOOR. You… translate?

VOGT. Our officers, they don't have much English. Or any other language, in truth. But I was lucky enough to vacation in England a while ago.

She smokes, watching him closely.

And I've lived in Paris for some time but… I don't think I know Paris so well as you do.

He looks through a paper on his desk.

The first woman they sent here to operate wireless… That's an honour.

So how is it you've lasted so long? Longer than any other 'pianist'…

Nothing.

Knowing how your SOE… recruits. How they seek out people with ties, prior lives, even, in the places they're sent to… I think… you must have connections… deep roots here in Paris.

NOOR. What… like an apricot tree?

VOGT. If you like.

4. The Firstborn

Suresnes, summer 1937, in the Oriental Room. MAMS *is putting lipstick on* NOOR.

MAMS. I queued an hour and a half at the pharmacy in Saint-Germain-des-Prés.

NOOR. What – ?!

MAMS. It's entirely worth it, you'll see.

What time are you meeting him?

NOOR. Six o'clock.

MAMS. Does Amma know?

NOOR *shakes her head.*

Have a look.

NOOR *looks at herself in a mirror and smiles.*

And…

MAMS *kisses her hand and leaves no mark.* NOOR *tries doing the same.*

Look! Not a trace!

NOOR. I love it!

MAMS. You look like you had a great time.

BHAI *comes in.*

NOOR. We did, didn't we, Bhai? We went on horseback rides –

BHAI. When she wasn't holed away, writing.

NOOR. I can't keep *Le Figaro* waiting! It's my first, proper commission.

BHAI. We even tried skiing, Mams. And lots of long walks and talks…

NOOR *looks at* MAMS.

NOOR. I should go see Amma…

BHAI. Uncle's with her.

NOOR. Why?

BHAI (*doing an impression of Uncle*). 'The situation in India is escalating.'

He might have to go back.

MAMS. Oh, yes please!

BHAI. It sounds really bad.

NOOR. What's the latest?

BHAI. The Britishers are carving up the country – annexing the Burmese, setting Hindus against Muslims. But no one's admitting what they're really up to.

MAMS. Which is… what?

BHAI. Dividing us. Making us weaker, so they can conquer.

But Jinnah just… postures about his religious state. And Gandhiji… hiding away on his moral highground, refusing to eat.

NOOR. What do you want them to do? Take arms against the British?

BHAI. Anything more than this… pathetic show of resistance!

NOOR. Bhai! Have you forgotten everything Abba taught us? He wouldn't want them raising their hands in violence against / each other.

BHAI. But they can raise their colonising hands? Against poor, brown bodies?

NOOR. No, of course not.

MAMS *sits at the piano, starts playing something quietly.*

BHAI. Imagine we're talking about your Eli. Do you want him to just sit back and let the Germans do what / they're doing –

NOOR. Will you stop that? He's called Azeem now. As you well know.

And I'll tell you what he thinks when I get back.

AMMA *is at the door.*

AMMA. You're going out? You just arrived.

NOOR. I'll be back to make dinner, I just have to…

AMMA. Your brother told me you talked. In Switzerland.

BHAI. Oh, we talked, but…

AMMA. Can you two go and check if your uncle is staying to eat with us?

MAMA. It's okay, Babs, I can make dinner –

AMMA. Both of you. Upstairs, please.

BHAI. Of course, Amma.

They leave. MAMS *steals a look at* NOOR *as she goes.*

AMMA. You've caught the sun.

NOOR. Yes, the light… bounces off the snow with such force –

AMMA. I used to love tanning. On the beach in San Francisco. I spent whole days doing nothing but soaking in the sunlight. Then I met your father and one of the first things he said… was how beautiful he found my… lovely fair skin.

NOOR. You are beautiful, Amma.

AMMA. Well, I've never been good enough for your uncles. They despised me the moment your abba brought me home.

NOOR. Who cares about them! Abba loved you and you loved him.

AMMA. I love him.

But to know you'll never be good enough. After going against my whole family… to marry your abba.

And now to have them… coming into my private quarters, sneering more than ever… 'You have no control over your daughter. Look at her, running around with a Jew, bringing shame on us all.'

They say his mother works in a laundry.

NOOR. She owns a laundry.

AMMA *takes* NOOR*'s hands in hers.*

AMMA. You're my firstborn. No matter how old you are, you'll always be my baby.

And your heart's so big. Just like your abba's.

NOOR. I love Azeem. Just like you love Abba.

AMMA. My Babuli. You're so young. And you descend from greatness… From emperors… Never forget that.

This Jew… He's not for you.

NOOR. I'm twenty-three, Amma. How old were you, when you left America, your home, everything you knew… to be with Abba?

AMMA. This boy is not your destiny.

She tucks a lock of hair behind NOOR*'s ear.*

You know that in your heart, don't you?

Don't you.

AMMA *kisses her on the head and leaves her.*

5. The Refugee

The upper deck of the Kasongo, *en route to Falmouth, England. 19 June 1940. A canopy of stars above.*

NOOR, *wrapped in a blanket, retches loudly over the side of the boat. Then gingerly heads back to* BHAI, *also hunched under a blanket.*

BHAI. Any better?

NOOR. Well, I vomited three / times –

BHAI. I don't want to / know –

NOOR. You asked, so… there's nothing left in me any more. And I do feel better, thank you!

BHAI.…There's a bit…

He points at the corner of her mouth and she wipes it with the back of her hand.

NOOR. You need to go down, check on Amma and / Mams.

BHAI. You want me to move?!

NOOR. Yes – !

BHAI. We're pitching a hundred and eighty degrees! And these… bloody beetles everywhere!

He feels something crawling up his neck and slaps at it. She finds this hilarious.

What?!

NOOR. You! I'm sorry.

I'll go see them in a minute. But first…

With a flourish, she pulls two cigarettes and some matches out of a pocket.

BHAI. Babsy, you miracle!

He throws his arms around her.

Where the hell did you get these?

NOOR. One for me, one for you.

She puts one in his mouth, then hers, and lights his first. As she lights his she sings:

Joyeux anniversaire, my little Bhai… Joyeux anniversaire!

She hugs him, then lights her own and they smoke a little while in contented silence, taking in the stars.

BHAI. Where's my birthday poem?

NOOR. I will… finish it as soon as we arrive.

BHAI. I'm joking.

NOOR (*pulling her notebook out from under her shawl*). No, I've a first draft here, look, and I'll get you a final / draft –

BHAI. Babs, Babs, I was pulling your leg! This is more than enough. You. A Gauloise.

And look… what I rammed in my pocket as we were leaving.

He pulls out a book. Her book, Twenty Jātaka Tales.

NOOR. Bhai! Thank you.

BHAI. Of course. It's a treasure.

Your own book. The first of many to come.

He opens the front cover and reads.

'For my Azeem. My sunrise.'

NOOR. Yes, well… he gave it back, when –

BHAI *hands it over to her and she holds it carefully with her notebook.*

BHAI. You made the right decision.

NOOR. Please don't say I told you so.

BHAI. I'm not.

NOOR. And I didn't do it because of you, okay?

BHAI. Okay.

Thank God, though. That we're safely out of that hell.

She tucks the notebook and book away.

NOOR. Are we?

BHAI. What do you mean?

NOOR. We're stateless, homeless… chucking our guts up into the Bay of Biscay –

BHAI. We're not / stateless –

NOOR. You heard them on the docks – refugees they called us.

They might not take us in.

BHAI. I have a passport!

NOOR. I don't! So what makes me any different from the thousands of… pathetic souls washing up on their shores?

BHAI. The English are kind, welcoming people.

A beat.

NOOR. Mams wakes up every night screaming.

BHAI. You think she wouldn't have screamed herself hoarse when the Germans break through our front gate, the sanctuary Abba built, ready to gun it all down?

NOOR. What do we do when we get there?

BHAI. Listen, don't worry about your passport, / it'll be –

NOOR. I don't mean that. What will we do? With ourselves? We can't just sit back and let these people… We have to do something, we have to, because…

For the first time in my life, I think human beings can be evil, and I can't… Is that bad?

He looks at her, processing things.

BHAI. I'm glad Abba's not here to see this.

A moment.

NOOR. Bhai, have you ever wondered… if he is still here?

Maybe just… hiding away somewhere in the Himalayas. After his whole life giving so much. To everyone else.

Sometimes I'd imagine him… sitting cross-legged in a cave, his beard long and grey now, meditating on the Bhagavad Gita.

But when the apricot tree started to wither…

They say, don't they, when the guru dies, the tree that gave him shade also… And seeing the termites devour it slowly, inside out… I nearly got an axe to chop it down, into a hundred thousand pieces.

He takes her hand.

Can you imagine killing someone?

BHAI *shakes his head.*

BHAI. You?

NOOR. Not even a Nazi.

But we've got to do something.

BHAI. I was thinking… of joining the RAF –

NOOR. Yes, you've always wanted to fly!

BHAI. If they'll have me.

NOOR. Well, they won't have me with my total terror of heights.

BHAI. In Bordeaux, they were talking about minesweepers. I could do that. It's dangerous, but no one'll actually put a gun in my hand.

NOOR. They'll surely have active roles for women, won't they? With everything –

BHAI. I bet they're desperate for nurses.

NOOR. I don't mean nursing.

BHAI. Why? You're wonderful at taking care of others.

NOOR. Bhai, I'm not wandering around, doling out spoonfuls of syrup if you're up in the skies risking your life. If we do this we're doing it. Together, / properly!

BHAI. No, Babs. You're not putting yourself at risk. I won't have it.

Amma needs you.

A beat.

We'll do our bit. Then we can all go home.

NOOR. Home? Without Abba's tree…

What did you use to say? That we lived our lives as if…?

BHAI. Looking out through stained-glass windows.

She takes in the stars, the moon, the wide sea.

NOOR. Not any more.

6. Nora Baker Part 3

Paris, 13 October 1943. NOOR *still sitting in* VOGT*'s office in avenue Foch.*

VOGT. So it was Prosper… and, specifically, the cell belonging to Cinema, you were sent to join.

And it's been three months since we infiltrated and shut it down. Your old network… Cinema, Archambault, Vaudevire. We rounded them up.

But somehow you remained. Alone. Transmitting… constantly. Our detection continued to pick up signals from Poste Madeleine.

You've sustained relations back to London. Back to your headquarters.

Still nothing

At 64 Baker Street… They must have trained you very well at Wanborough, then Beaulieu –

NOOR. How… do you…? Do you… have an agent in London?

VOGT. I try to do my job as well as you have been doing yours.

NOOR. I know you and your jobs. Translator! Just be honest and say it, you're going to torture me, I've heard all about your… vile / ways…

VOGT. No torture happens here. No one will torture you here.

NOOR. Do you think I'm stupid?

VOGT. Not at all.

A small beat.

NOOR. I'm sorry but I have to take a bath.

VOGT. Excuse me?

NOOR. Before I talk… I need a bath.

VOGT. You'll certainly have ample time to wash and do all of that after dinner –

NOOR. I want to do it now. You said yourself, I've been on the run a long time. It's only dignified I should be allowed to be clean.

VOGT. Certainly. One of my officers will show you where the bathroom is.

7. The Recruit

London, October 1942. A small room in the Victoria Hotel. NOOR *stands facing* JEPSON. *She's smartly turned out, her hair freshly set.*

JEPSON. Nora.

NOOR. That's it.

JEPSON. Where are you at the moment?

NOOR. Right now?

She looks around her.

JEPSON. Don't be smart with me.

NOOR. I wasn't –

JEPSON. Serving. Where are you serving at the moment?

NOOR. With the WAAF.

JEPSON. For the last… two years –

NOOR. Two years, yes.

JEPSON. You signed on with your brother?

NOOR. Yes, my brother joined the RAF, / and –

JEPSON. You've received training on the wireless?

NOOR. I have.

JEPSON. We have been teaching you to send secret, coded messages.

NOOR. You have.

JEPSON. Then what on earth is this in your file about Russia?

NOOR. Russia?

JEPSON. Yes, good God, woman, will you stop that! Is that all you know to do? To parrot what you hear?

NOOR. No.

JEPSON. No, what? I am your superior officer.

NOOR. No, sir.

JEPSON. You need to tell me about your ties to Russia.

NOOR. I don't know what you mean, sir.

JEPSON. You don't? (*Eyeing her.*) You do know you were born in Moscow?

NOOR. We left when I was a few months old.

JEPSON. How many?

NOOR. I, goodness, let me think… Almost a year, I think. The Great War was just starting –

JEPSON. When have you been back since?

NOOR. Never.

JEPSON. Have you any ties there still?

NOOR. I do not.

JEPSON. Have you ever used a British military wireless set to communicate with agents in Russia?

NOOR. No.

JEPSON. Because you realise how grave, how significant the punishment for that / would be?

NOOR. I have not. I would not.

He holds her gaze.

Is this an interrogation, sir?

JEPSON. How about your father? The Indian.

NOOR.…My father died when I was thirteen.

JEPSON. Whilst on a trip back to India.

Why was he there?

NOOR. I believe he felt a need to go home.

JEPSON. Home?

Do you believe as fervently, as passionately as he, about Indian independence? Or indeed, as did your great-great-grandfather, the mighty Tiger of Mysore, Tipu Sultan?

NOOR. One more great.

JEPSON. I'm sorry?

NOOR. I'm his great-great-great granddaughter.

A moment.

JEPSON. So you are of royal lineage…

There was much debate around your fitness for service.

NOOR. Your colleagues decreed and I have it in writing –
I am a British Protected Person. I have the right to serve.
And defend –

JEPSON. But what are you? Indian or English?

A silence.

NOOR. Or French? Even Russian?

JEPSON *eyes her.*

There's a story my father would tell. He was a very wise man.

JEPSON. Was he – ?

NOOR. If you'll permit me… sir.

He gives no indication of yes or no.

Three men are in a blacked-out room. They're trying to discover the identity of some vast object in the room with them.

One says: it's long, thin and very bendy, like a huge hose. Another says: it's so large I cannot reach across it with both hands – it's a wall. The third says: what do you mean? It's right next to me, planted on the floor here and I can wrap my arms around it in an embrace.

What do you think it was?

JEPSON. I'm sure you are going to tell me.

NOOR. Of course, each man was describing the different body parts of the same elephant.

We look different, feel different. But is that all we shall be judged upon?

I am at present a proud servant of Britain – I say of us, can our will be crushed? Perhaps suppressed momentarily, but I, you, all of us engaged, shall fight for it back, every acre of it. I'll go to the other end of the world but I'll fight for it back.

Can we not say the same of India?

He writes something down.

Your French is very good, sir.

JEPSON. Like you, I studied at the Sorbonne. Like you, I'm a writer.

NOOR.…I only write children's stories.

JEPSON. Stories all the same.

NOOR. Sir, I have asked for some time and was told you don't admit women into active service.

JEPSON. We didn't. But you'll be one of the first. I convinced the Prime Minister.

You see, your sex has far greater capacity for cool and lonely courage. Men need steadying and shoring up from a mate; you women, not so much.

A beat.

NOOR. I've shown courage in the past.

JEPSON. Good.

Because this lot'll stop at nothing – rifle butts, cigarette butts, injections of God only knows what concocted in the room next door.

He stands.

NOOR. I'm one of the first?

JEPSON. To my mind, the most precious skill for the service into which we're engaging you is your writer's… vivid capacity to imagine the unknown. To reshape narratives… oneself, even.

NOOR. So you're engaging me? Is this… all there is / to it?

JEPSON. There will be training –

NOOR. Of / course.

JEPSON. – but otherwise, yes.

I knew it as soon as you walked in the room.

8. The Friend

Wanborough Manor, near Guildford. Early March 1943. YOLANDE *is massaging* NOOR*'s feet as she scribbles away in her notebook* (*the same we saw on the* Kasongo).

The sound of ample laughter bleeds in from a nearby room.

YOLANDE. What do you write in there? I see you carrying it everywhere.

NOOR.…Notes, stories… Things that need to be preserved.

YOLANDE. Stories?

NOOR. I… used to be a writer. Before all this. But please don't tell any of / them –

YOLANDE. Nora! How clever!

NOOR. No, not / at all –

YOLANDE. Can I read something?

NOOR. I don't have anything ready to share but… I started something yesterday.

YOLANDE. What's it about?

NOOR. The main character's called Snowdrop.

YOLANDE. How funny.

A moment.

NOOR. When I was little… I used to see fairies. Actually… see them. In the flowers in our garden. I'd walk along saying, good morning, good afternoon to them, and they'd… sing their little hellos back.

Then one day, this Dutch woman who had come to see my father… I don't remember exactly what she said but I do remember she had an incredibly large forehead… It was something like, 'Oh she's just being silly, she's just imagining it' and…

YOLANDE. She took them away from you.

NOOR. From then on, the flowers were… empty. I used to sleepwalk as a child but… I never did after that.

YOLANDE. Nora.

NOOR. We trust each other, don't we, Yolande?

YOLANDE. Of course.

NOOR. Sometimes I'm so terrified. Of what's ahead. The stories. Of toenails being pulled out.

And I… I write silly, children's fairy tales for goodness' sake! I just –

What on earth was I thinking, that I could do this?

YOLANDE. Of course you can / do this.

NOOR. I barely finished the training run today.

YOLANDE. Didn't you see how the Major looked at your target this morning? You had more hits than most of the boys.

NOOR. Yes but – when we're really there. What they could do…

YOLANDE. The way I see it… It won't be my decision if a German tries to kill me. They might kill me physically. But that's all.

They won't win anything. They'll just have a dead body, useless to them. But they will not have *me*. I won't let them.

My word, these feet are so tiny!

YOLANDE *picks up her sewing.*

NOOR. Really! How many evenings do you spend stitching their socks?!

YOLANDE. I mean, they're so totally useless, but if I didn't who would?

NOOR. Oh let them get blisters! We do!

A roar as two drunken SOLDIERS *come carousing in.*

SOLDIER 2. Girls. Girls! What on / earth…?

SOLDIER 1. What the devil's this?

SOLDIER 2. Madeleine and Mariette… abandoning us for the comforts of each other, / it seems!

YOLANDE. Well, you seemed perfectly taken up with the very liberal attention of that waitress.

SOLDIER 1. Oh!! Someone's jealous!

YOLANDE. / What?!

NOOR. You wish! She's engaged to a wonderful man.

SOLDIER 2 *looms over* YOLANDE.

SOLDIER 2. Come on, Mariette! What's a little engagement between friends? After all that help I gave you on the assault / course.

YOLANDE. Don't touch me.

She gives SOLDIER 2 *a push and he stumbles.*

SOLDIER 2. Bloody hell!

SOLDIER 1. Man down! Revive him, Mariette!

YOLANDE. In your dreams.

SOLDIER 1. He needs the kiss of life!

YOLANDE. Go call your waitress.

SOLDIER 1 (*grabbing* YOLANDE). No, he needs you!

YOLANDE (*caught in his hold*). You know it's all a test, don't you? Sending a beautiful woman to pour your wine and stroke your cheek. Major Wesselow's watching from the bar to see if she manages to loosen your tongue –

NOOR. Or your trousers –

YOLANDE. And if she does, the game's over, my boy.

SOLDIER 2. You'll look after me, won't you, Madeleine? Or are you engaged too?

NOOR *looks at him, impassive.*

SOLDIER 1. I hear she's a princess. Out of your league, old chum.

SOLDIER 2. Every princess ought to kiss a frog one day…

NOOR *walks up to* SOLDIER 2 *and kisses him squarely and slowly.*

SOLDIER 1. Madeleine!!

NOOR. You might have a kiss, but you'll never have me.

She pushes him back to the ground and goes back to YOLANDE.

YOLANDE. You're a princess?

MAJOR WESSELOW *comes striding in. They all scrabble to stand to attention.*

/ Sir.

NOOR. Sir.

WESSELOW. Howatt! Get up off the floor!

SOLDIER 2. Yes, sir.

WESSELOW. And, Madeleine – you aren't wearing any shoes.

NOOR. No, sir, I –

WESSELOW. Is it some kind of… cultural practice?

NOOR. No, sir. I've just got an awful blister after yesterday's / drill.

WESSELOW. I'd get them on quicksmart if I were you. One test is over; time for the next. We're heading out over the Hog's Back / – night exercise.

YOLANDE. Now, / sir?!

SOLDIER 2. It's pitch black out there!

WESSELOW. Yes.

NOOR. Sir, the chaps… some of them are pretty…

WESSELOW. What?

NOOR. I think they've had a bit to drink, sir.

WESSELOW. Do you think the enemy will only opt to launch an attack, that you'll only be required to beat an escape or fire your weapon, during the hours of daylight? When stone cold sober?

NOOR. No, sir.

WESSELOW. Then get those bloody shoes on and out! On the double.

NOOR *scrabbles to get her shoes on. Tucks her notebook out of sight. They arrive at the range, alongside a handful of other recruits.*

They shoot. NOOR *working closer and closer to the centre of her target.*

9. The Trailblazer

London, mid-May 1943. Manetta's restaurant in Mayfair. NOOR *reads a letter as* VERA *watches her, a martini in front of her.*

NOOR. My… fitness? For the job?

Why would someone write this?

VERA. You tell me.

NOOR. Who was it?

A small beat.

VERA. Your conducting officer. And given she's overseen your progress thus far –

NOOR. Yes… all the reports from Wanborough, on the firearms, and my improvements in PT?

VERA. There's no denying, Nora, the huge progress you've made, physically… with the technical aspects of your training

NOOR. But you're to negate all that, Miss Atkins, on the grounds of one woman's testimony?

VERA. Nora, please… call me Vera.

A beat.

What you're about to undertake – this is far greater than a technical exercise.

Do you understand how dangerous the work will be? How much you will need physically, mentally, to stay out of the grasp of German detection? Being required to lie time and time again to cover any tracks. Your… moral obligation to the truth – is cause for concern, / given –

NOOR. I will not lie. But what if I just… say nothing?

VERA. What do you mean?

NOOR *looks at her – a long beat of silence.*

NOOR. I hold my truth… and they don't get what they want.

A tiny beat.

VERA. The current lifespan of an operator is six weeks.

This officer is concerned not about your technical skill but about your… internal resources. To last out your time.

VERA *takes the letter and reads from it.*

'She has descended into a gloom… Clearly troubled by what she is about to undertake.'

Tell me about this.

NORA. It's true. What she says. But it's not fear.

What she calls here… my 'childlike' qualities. Gentle manner… Lack of ruse… Do you think she knows me, Miss Atkins, more than I know myself?

VERA. But you do appreciate that your… beliefs, having been raised a Muslim, a pacifist –

NORA. Were you raised a Sufi, Miss Atkins?

VERA. I was not.

NOOR. Do you know the beliefs we hold? Could you describe them to me in their full, rich complexity?

VERA. No.

NOOR. Yet you can presume to know how my beliefs will play out in my person?

A beat.

VERA. You just said it's true. What she writes here?

NOOR.…It's my mother.

It's leaving her…

When my father died… I was the one who held her together. And I think it would break her if…

VERA. Yes. So what do we do?

You see, there's only one crime: to go out there and let your comrades down.

10. Nora Baker Part 4

Paris, 13 October 1943. VOGT *sits at his desk flicking through* NOOR*'s notebook.* NOOR *comes in fired up.*

VOGT. What's going / on?

NOOR. Your guard is trying to hold the door open with a brick. And he doesn't understand a word I'm saying to him.

VOGT. I did tell you.

NOOR. He'll be able to see me while I'm bathing – I need to undress, clean myself, properly.

I have to be able to close the door.

VOGT. Alright.

VOGT *goes out and comes back.*

He has taken the brick away.

But so you understand, I have gone against the Sturmbannführer's orders. For you.

She goes. VOGT *looks through* NOOR*'s notebooks and papers. Then the sound of loud banging offstage, like someone trying to break a door down.*

GUARD (*off*). Miss, miss! You must open. Miss!

Then a loud crash of the door giving way.

She's a fucking escape artist! She's out on the roof!

VOGT *springs up and races out.*

VOGT. What?!

NOOR *has climbed out of the window. Five storeys up. She feels her way along the gutter. Stops to gather her nerve.*

VOGT *eases his way out of a window near, but not too near, her.*

Madeleine, don't be crazy!

You're fifty feet from the ground.

NOOR. I'm not stupid.

VOGT. Believe me, I know that.

She inches away from him.

NOOR. And I'm not scared.

VOGT. I know that too.

So what's your plan?

Officers will be up on this roof very soon.

NOOR. I've had so much practice running from your officers.

VOGT. Just now, you spoke of torture – I promise you… on my children's heads, no torture ever happens here.

But you do this, you try to escape, and my chief imprisons you somewhere else… there's no such promise.

She inches away a bit further.

NOOR. I don't want anything you promise.

She continues her steady inching away. She loses her footing slightly, then composes herself.

VOGT. You lied just now.

You said you were going to take a bath. I thought you are a person of honour, but / I was –

NOOR. You dare speak of honour, when your people are / doing –

Her foot slips and she just catches herself. He leans out, almost in a whisper:

VOGT. Madeleine, please – you will kill yourself. Please don't.

Think of your mother. You want to get back to your mother, don't you? Don't you?

Give me your hand.

11. La Petite Mère

London, end of May 1943. Ameena Begum's home in Taviton Street. AMMA *sits in her chair and* NOOR *holds her hand.*

AMMA. Let's take a look at you.

NOOR *stands, straightens out her skirt.*

Oh, lovely. And who is it you're deployed with now?

MAMS. The FANYs, Mum.

AMMA. What's that?

NOOR. Nursing Yeomanry.

She sees what MAMS *is holding – a glass of water and some pills.*

No, Mams, it's two a day. One in the morning, one at night.

MAMS. So why are there so many?

NOOR. I picked up extra. Save you a job.

AMMA. La petite mère. Keeping us all in check.

MAMS. I'll manage just fine, you / know.

NOOR. I know.

AMMA *takes her tablet with a drink of water. Over the next lines* MAMS *goes to the piano and plays a variation on 'Clair de Lune'.*

AMMA. And have they said how long?

NOOR. Six weeks. Maybe longer.

AMMA. So they're sending you somewhere far off?

NOOR. To be honest… I don't know. Official secrets and all / that.

MAMS. You must have some idea.

NOOR. I think it might be Africa.

AMMA. Good heavens! There'll be rougher types there, / I know it.

MAMS. Amma!

AMMA. Why are they putting you in danger's way like this? I don't think it's right.

NOOR. We're doing jobs the boys can't, Amma. And the girls I'm with, we're all… of a very superior type. We've been handpicked – imagine that. What times these are!

AMMA. What can I say? I wish you weren't going.

NOOR *kneels at* AMMA*'s feet and kisses her hands.*

NOOR. I love you as high as the sky. As wide as the universe.

A moment.

AMMA. Your abba met Debussy, you know?

MAMS. I think you've told us once or twice before.

NOOR. I'm going to have to…

MAMS. Already?

She stops playing.

I'm walking you down to the square.

NOOR. No, Mams, you don't need / to.

MAMS. I want to.

NOOR. Look, they've promised to write about how we're getting on, so you'll get plenty of news. And I'll send little cards whenever I can…

And when it's all over, we'll hop back on that boat… fewer beetles this time, let's hope! Back to Suresnes…

We'll spend all our days in the garden… up in the Oriental Room, us on the piano and you can just relax in peace, have a little sing-along.

A beat.

AMMA. I don't know what it is but you look…

NOOR. What?

AMMA. Doesn't she?

MAMS. My word, yes!

NOOR. What do you mean?

AMMA. There are diamonds… in your eyes. What's happened?

NOOR. Nothing! I don't know! I feel… I'm on the right path, / I suppose.

MAMS. Do / you?!

NOOR. To be doing something… at last. That counts.

AMMA *looks at her.*

AMMA. Yes. I see it.

And your abba knew. That night, escaping Moscow.

NOOR. Knew what?

AMMA. Mams, you weren't there, but I tell you… I'd never known fear like it. We had to get out, your abba, Babs and me… Everyone was wild with panic.

But not everyone had a sled lent to them by / the great Tolstoy.

MAMS. / The Great Tolstoy. No!

NOOR. The Great Tolstoy.

AMMA. But even in Leo's magnificent sled, we got stuck. They'd blockaded the frontiers.

And your abba knew… He rose up, his hair and robes billowing in the cold light. He lifted you from my arms, bundled up like a tiny baby rabbit, held you up high… high above the crowd.

Everything stopped. Everyone went quiet. The soldiers opened the barricades and let us all pass.

That was you.

A beat.

MAMS. Above all those people?

AMMA. Yes!

MAMS. She was a baby.

AMMA. Our first.

MAMS. Why did you… let him?

AMMA. What do you mean?

MAMS. Why did you let him take her?

AMMA. All those people made way. So many lives were saved.

Because of her.

NOOR.…Weren't you scared?

AMMA. Of what?

NOOR. I was… so little. All those desperate, angry people all around.

Weren't you… scared? That I might fall?

12. Jeanne-Marie

Tangmere Airfield, West Sussex, 16 June 1943. Under a full moon.

VERA *does her final checks – labels on the back of* NOOR*'s blouse, skirt, jacket.*

NOOR. I suppose this isn't the time to invoke how terrified I am of heights?

VERA. It is not.

Now remember… for you, this is a return to home; for Jeanne-Marie Renier, it is not. She is ignorant of everything you know – the best places for coffee, the people you called friends. Yes?

NOOR. Yes.

VERA. And please always… extreme care with filing your messages.

NOOR. With the filing, yes.

VERA. Under all the pressures… finding secure locations, transmitting undetected… you must pay the utmost attention. Everything filed carefully.

NOOR. Roger that.

The sounds of an airplane. The brooch on VERA*'s lapel catches* NOOR*'s eye.*

You're so clever, Vera – even in the extremest circumstances, you always wear something pretty.

VERA *unpins it and pins it to* NOOR*'s lapel.*

No!

VERA. Yes. Something to send you off with.

NOOR. Thank you.

VERA. This blue really is your colour.

So, on landing…

NOOR. I'll make my way straight to Paris. Directly to… Cinema's apartment.

VERA. He and his sister are expecting you tomorrow. They've accessed a radio for you to confirm your safe arrival –

NOOR. And you'll notify me where and when my own set will be dropped?

VERA. Within a week.

Final bits, then? Identity card number:

NOOR *roots through her satchel and takes out her identity card.*

Without looking.

NOOR. Vingt-quatre, deux, quarante-trois.

VERA. Yes, Mademoiselle Renier.

NOOR. Enchantée.

VERA. And where were you born?

NOOR. In Blois, twenty-fifth April 1918. Now a children's nurse. Daughter of Auguste Renier, philosophy professor, and Ray Baker, American by birth, French by marriage.

VERA. Thus explaining your somewhat singular accent.

NOOR. Indeed.

VERA. You have your ration card?

NOOR (*taking it out of her satchel*). Paris sixteenth, dated thirtieth December 1941.

She puts the ration card back and takes out a small, stubby pistol, holding it tenderly.

And… my little hunk of dynamite.

VERA. I hear you're really quite the shot now.

And your lipstick case?

NOOR *tucks the gun back away, takes out a lipstick case and from it, carefully handles some pills.*

NOOR. One, two, three and four.

VERA. Now… once again, please – that L-pill…

NOOR. What about it?

VERA. It is no joke.

A moment.

NOOR. What do you mean?

VERA. It is only for situations of utmost peril. And we worry –

NOOR. We?!

VERA. – I worry… you might misinterpret, mistake things to be worse than they actually / are –

NOOR. And what…? Swallow cyanide by mistake?

VERA. No…

NOOR. Do you all think me silly? A silly little coward?

VERA. No, but you have no safety net. No uniform to protect you. In situations of incredible / risk –

NOOR. I know that.

VERA. If they capture you –

NOOR. Yes, I am very aware.

In the distance, the propellers of a Lysander roar into action. NOOR *handles the four pills with care back into the lipstick case.*

The roar of the engines sound as the plane taxis nearer. NOOR *loses herself in the noise, the light, the sensation of the wind.*

VERA. Right then. Looks like Bunny's ready for you. It's a ludicrous name really, for a pilot. And such a gorgeous one…

VERA *notices that* NOOR *is staring, watching the plane, motionless.*

Madeleine.

Madeleine…

She goes to her and places a firm hand on her shoulder. NOOR *turns and holds both* VERA*'s hands tightly.*

Madeleine, / are you –

NOOR. Miss Atkins, Vera, I beg you… Please remember… my mother.

VERA. You have my word.

VERA *straightens her suit.*

Right then.

NOOR. No fame or name.

VERA. What's that?

NOOR (*over the roar*)….No fame or name, Vera.

I think… I understand now.

She walks into the light of the Lysander – the roar of the engine grows and grows to blackout.

End of Act One.

ACT TWO

1. Nora Baker Part 5

Paris, 31 October 1943. VOGT*'s office in avenue Foch. He hands over a sheet of paper.*

VOGT. Help me with this transmission you made in July.

NOOR. You ask so nicely, Ernest, but you know I won't.

VOGT. We'll try, shall we?

I'm interested in this one because here we have names of the agents you arranged to be returned to England by Lysander in July –

NOOR. Yes but… those agents are long gone and safely landed in England.

VOGT. Right.

And they were collected by… 'Bunny'?

NOOR. Yes.

Fine, I will tell you something. It was Bunny who flew me in to France.

VOGT. In June?

NOOR. Yes, the month before. June seventeenth, full moon.

VOGT *scribbles a note.*

And I'll tell you something else… That he was very handsome.

VOGT. Was he?

NOOR. Very.

VOGT. So then a mere few weeks after you arrived, you sent this message arranging another flight for Bunny, to come and collect two agents and their 'basket of cherries'.

What is that?

NOOR. A basket of cherries?

VOGT. Yes.

NOOR. Exactly what it says it is.

Now, what I wouldn't give for a proper clafoutis…

VOGT. Nora.

NOOR. There's one more thing I can tell you. That clafoutis was my favourite dessert as a child.

He shakes his head.

VOGT. I think the 'basket of cherries' might have been some kind of ammunition – is that right? And if so, why were the agents transporting arms out of France? Who were you sending them to?

NOOR. I can tell you… that it was not ammunition.

VOGT. So what was it?

Nothing.

You know, it seems… such a waste you came on this terrible mission. You are an exceptionally intelligent, gifted girl. You could have done so many interesting, valuable things at home.

NOOR. If I had to make the choice again, I would make it the same.

VOGT. But you realise we have the French Section three-quarters mopped up? That your sacrifice will not have counted for much.

NOOR. I have served my country. That is my recompense.

He turns back to her papers.

VOGT. Well… let's try something else. I want your help identifying some persons of interest. Let's start with Vaudevire. Who are they and what did they do?

NOOR. You know this is something I will not tell you.

VOGT. There are so many names in your notebook. Code names, cover names… Some of them are surely part of the French Section. And Resistant groups.

But perhaps others are… simple people. Who rendered you small services – lodgings or allowing you to use their home for… whatever purpose. Out of friendship.

If you don't tell me enough to enable us to distinguish between them, we shall be obliged to arrest them all. And my officers will find them all in the end.

Like we found you.

And those friends… who've done so little, hardly at all understanding what they were doing in showing you kindness, will suffer with those who were important.

But if you tell me which ones are responsible agents of any Resistance organisations, I promise you – none of the others will be touched.

Her hands start to jitter again. She looks about.

Now, these names again. Vaudevire? Gieules? Louis Deux?

2. Rolande 1

Paris, mid-August 1943. A small apartment on rue Hautefeuille belonging to VIENNOT. *Homely.*

VIENNOT *is holding a smallish briefcase* – NOOR*'s set. His wife,* ELISABETH, *is bustling about getting ready to go out, coat on, etc.*

ELISABETH. Honestly, Pierre! I can't believe he hasn't offered – please take a coffee, Rolande.

NOOR. Really, I'm / fine.

ELISABETH. I insist.

She heads into the kitchen and clanks about.

I have two minutes then I must go. The children will be running rings around my mother!

NOOR. How many do you have?

A beat.

ELISABETH. Sorry? You were talking to me?

NOOR. Yes. How many children do you have?

ELISABETH. Two. Marc and Elodie.

NOOR. Ah! Boy then a girl – the king's choice!

ELISABETH. Yes, exactly! And you…?

NOOR. Oh, I've no children. Yet.

But it's something my fiancé and I talked about. Before the war. Let's see when it's all over.

ELISABETH. Yes.

A beat.

NOOR. It was very good of your husband to fix… my apparatus.

ELISABETH. Yes. You work in a cinema?

NOOR.…That's right.

ELISABETH. What joy! To be able to watch Jean Gabin as many times as you want.

He adored *Pépé le Moko*, didn't you?

NOOR. I love that film!

ELISABETH. It's not really my thing, but any excuse to stare into Gabin's / eyes.

VIENNOT. My love, shouldn't you…? Elodie will be screaming her head off by now.

ELISABETH. Yes, I suppose I should. Coffee's ready in five minutes.

She kisses him.

See you Monday.

NOOR. Thank you.

ELISABETH *goes.* VIENNOT *is a knot of rage.*

I'm sorry, I should have / called before –

VIENNOT. I don't believe – Do you normally just arrive like this, at a person's home?

NOOR. You said it would be ready today.

VIENNOT. And what the hell were you doing asking about my children, personal information –

NOOR. I didn't / think –

VIENNOT. Right! I mean, do you think? Do you have any idea? About the risks? That we're all taking? Fucking crazy English woman, I don't know who you are!

NOOR. Give me my radio and I'll go.

He hands the set over.

She walks to the door. Then turns back.

She started, actually. Talking about your children.

And you have no need to be so… disgracefully rude.

VIENNOT. Oh really!

NOOR. No, you don't! Just totally… uncivilised.

When I've given your team so much support! Sending messages to your people in London whenever you've needed. I've done that.

On top of everything my superiors require. And there's only me… You dare say I'm not to be trusted!

I don't think I'm the one who's fucking crazy, to be honest.

A beat.

VIENNOT. I shouldn't have said that.

NOOR. Yes, well… I'll leave you in / peace.

VIENNOT. It's okay. Look – the coffee's ready.

NOOR. No thank you.

VIENNOT. Vaudevire and Gieules did say. How much you've been helping.

A beat.

They also say you have nowhere to transmit.

NOOR. They've been driving me out to the countryside. Absolutely ridiculous, really, dangling my antenna out of the car window, on a country lane in Levallois –

VIENNOT. That is ridiculous.

NOOR. Not ideal.

VIENNOT. I suppose you need to confirm to your people you're back on your set. You can do it from here if you / like.

NOOR. No, it's fine.

VIENNOT. No, really.

I mean, I'll be very clear, I would never offer when my family are / here.

NOOR. Of course.

VIENNOT. But… she has gone, so…

NOOR. If you're sure?

VIENNOT. You'd better do it before I change my mind.

She is straight to it, getting the set out of the case, unfurling the antenna. As she does:

NOOR. I do need to send the intelligence Gieules found.

VIENNOT. About Orly? / Yes.

NOOR. Once they have the coordinates of the airport, the Allies'll bomb the life out of the Luftwaffe. And when they do…

A small moment as she works to untangle the antenna.

VIENNOT. Can I / help?

NOOR. I'm absolutely fine.

VIENNOT. You've really been working alone?

NOOR. Mm-hmm.

VIENNOT. Your cell… Cinema…

NOOR. Not even two weeks after I arrived, Gestapo swooped in, rounded everyone up.

I'd been staying with Cinema and his sister but, after the arrests… I was out on my own.

VIENNOT. Where did you go?

NOOR. I have… connections. In Paris.

She looks back at him. A little flicker of pride maybe. Then goes back to what she was doing, stretching to get the antenna over a curtain rail.

VIENNOT. You didn't want to go back to London?

NOOR. Oh, they tried to make me. Said it's too dangerous. But they need me here –

She overbalances and slips off the chair.

VIENNOT. Careful!

NOOR. Shit!

VIENNOT. Shhhhhhh!

NOOR (*whispering*). I'm so sorry!

He pads to the door, listening for any sound outside the apartment. Then takes the antenna from her.

VIENNOT. Just… let me?

She lets him. He gets on the chair and extends the antenna out the window as she holds it steady.

NOOR. I'll be ten minutes, absolute maximum.

VIENNOT. Okay.

NOOR. Will you… keep look out, while I'm transmitting? You don't really want me staring out your window, do you?

VIENNOT. No, I don't.

NOOR. If you see a van, or one of their thugs with the earpieces…

He steps down and they take each other in.

Well, I suppose you are… tall, aren't you?

VIENNOT. You're… not so tall.

NOOR. No.

He slides the chair away. With a loud scrape.

Careful!

He composes himself.

VIENNOT. I'll get the –

He goes to the kitchen. She settles herself at the table, notebook, etc. He comes back with a cup.

Why do they call you Rolande?

NOOR. No idea. It was Gieules who chose it.

Why do they call you Louis Deux?

VIENNOT. Well… if I have too much cognac, I s–, s– some–some–… sometimes –

NOOR. You…

VIENNOT. His nickname was the Stammerer.

NOOR. That's terrible!

She drinks the coffee in one go. Pulls a face.

VIENNOT. It's not good?

NOOR. It's… fine!

VIENNOT. You are a terrible liar.

And Gieules's an idiot. You look nothing like Rolande.

NOOR. No?

VIENNOT. Not at all. Rolande is a… large, doughy woman. With fat fingers. But those… (*Looking at her hands.*)

Those are the hands of a pianist – (*He means it in the WW2 sense: wireless op.*)

NOOR. Well, I am! An actual pianist. Like, on the piano.

VIENNOT. Really?

NOOR. Do you know Debussy?

VIENNOT. I'm not sure… Is he one of Vaudevire's guys?

She cracks up.

NOOR. No! That's a story for another day.

I should…

She turns her focus to her set.

VIENNOT. What is… all this you have written?

NOOR. My notes. Everything filed carefully.

VIENNOT. Surely you cannot – you never keep anything on paper / such as –

NOOR. I'm sorry but we don't have time to chat. That wire's hanging / out your window –

VIENNOT. Of course.

NOOR. Watch the clock. Tell me when eight minutes have passed.

VIENNOT. Ready when you are.

She starts tapping away on the key on her set, completely focused. There should be some sort of music. The fusion of her art and her fight.

VIENNOT *watches out the window, watches her at work, checking his watch.*

3. Rolande 2

Paris, late September 1943. A hotel room near Gare Saint-Lazare.

VIENNOT *sits in a chair with* NOOR*'s set at his feet, watching her sleep. From total stillness, she wakes with a gasp.*

VIENNOT. It's here, I've got it.

Seeing the set is safe, she lies back down, closes her eyes for another moment. Then:

NOOR. What time is it?

VIENNOT. You slept… not even two hours. Rest / some more.

NOOR. The time, Pierre?

VIENNOT. Eleven forty-five.

She hauls herself up and goes to a jug, pours water into her hands and splashes it into her face.

NOOR (*calling to him*). My sked's twelve fifteen, I have to / get to it –

VIENNOT. Shhhh.

Wiping her face with a towel, she sits on the edge of the bed. Tired to the bone, her hands play the phantom piano – chords echo in her head. He sits next to her. After a moment.

NOOR. I wish I was with my mother.

VIENNOT. Can't you just… transmit later? You need to sleep.

NOOR. It can't wait, Pierre. The Canadians are getting somewhere, finally, building up the northern network; London need Gieules to connect them with your people up there. If I'm not on time, the whole operation could fall apart –

VIENNOT. It won't fall apart, Gieules can handle it.

NOOR. No, London need / to know!

VIENNOT. London have abandoned you / here –

NOOR. No one's abandoned me!

They keep telling me to get on the next Lysander back.

VIENNOT. Then why the hell don't you?

NOOR. Oh, so you want me to go?

VIENNOT. Of course not.

NOOR. I can't leave all of you here, without –

VIENNOT. You cannot do the work of a whole circuit, alone.

NOOR. I can. I have been!

VIENNOT. Madeleine is not more important than… whoever you were before this.

NOOR. But she is.

This is.

A moment.

All my life, I've hated following rules… Don't eat chocolates before dinnertime. You must call him sir…

I've had to be a good girl. A responsible girl. And I don't want to any more.

You know… when you play a piece of music… of course the notes are there – the dots and dashes, in black and white. But when you play… you can do anything. The music… flies… when you find movement and breath and… your own voice.

Do you know what I mean?

He takes her hands.

Why did you kiss me? In the hotel reception.

VIENNOT. I wanted them to believe that we are…

NOOR. …What?

VIENNOT. Lovers, escaping the world for a few hours.

NOOR. And what if we were?

He touches her face. They kiss and are carried off on a few long moments. Finally:

VIENNOT. Somehow, these days, you have become a real Parisienne. No longer the little English girl.

NOOR. I am a Parisienne. A Surenois.

She kisses him again.

VIENNOT. Listen to me, please, you have to stop going back there, to Suresnes… Seeing your old friends. You're trusting too many people.

NOOR. Not you too! You sound like Miss Atkins.

VIENNOT. At least these English know something.

NOOR. But she doesn't know! They don't know… what we need.

One another, our own people, to get through this… nightmare.

VIENNOT. And what if the Gestapo come to your people, your old neighbour in Suresnes, and hold a gun to her head?

NOOR. She would never betray me!

You would never betray me.

He doesn't say anything. Her hands start to jitter again, searching for chords.

Open my case, will you? The pocket at the top.

VIENNOT *does. Takes out the lipstick case.*

Open it.

He does and takes out a pill.

VIENNOT. Is this…?

NOOR. Cyanide. In case we're captured.

I look at it every day… Even if I'm so scared that I feel entirely empty… I could never, ever swallow it.

Because the alternative… to being here, doing what we're doing, is unimaginably worse. Worse than death.

VIENNOT. My boy… Marc… We were walking past the Senate and he saw the flag flying high over the city, he asked, 'Papa, is that the flag of France?'

It was the swastika.

He's four years old. I will never accept this to be the world he lives in.

She strokes the frown lines on his brow. Kisses him.

4. Nora Baker Part 6

Paris, 31 October 1943. VOGT*'s office in avenue Foch. Just a few minutes on from Nora Baker 5.*

VOGT. Someone betrayed you.

NOOR. If you say so.

VOGT. In September, you were working with some 'Canadians'. You believed they were there to support your efforts in the north of France. But they were no more Canadian than I am.

Someone, in your network of les Resistants… capitulated and sent you to meet with us – 'The Canadians'. And we almost captured you…

NOOR. But you didn't.

VOGT. Who do you think it was? That betrayed you?

NOOR. Why should I believe you?

VOGT. By your honour you are protecting them; but they did not protect you.

A beat.

NOOR. Where's my set?

VOGT. It's downstairs.

NOOR. Why?

VOGT. You'll not answer my questions but you want me to answer yours.

She looks at him.

I don't know what they're doing with your transmitter downstairs. I can't answer because I don't know.

What do you fear? That they could be using it to communicate falsely with your people –

NOOR. Your funkspiel, everyone knows about it!

VOGT. Well yes, we can all play games, Nora.

But I need you to talk so that I can keep you here, safe and alive. I want to help you. That's not how others have been with you, I know that, but please believe it of me.

5. Rolande 3

Paris, September 1943. A café table on the edge of a busy street near Gare Saint-Lazare – a jolly statue of Gambrinus, the king of beer, holding a tankard aloft, hangs over them.

NOOR *is hunched over a cup of coffee; she is tiny with the fear.*

VIENNOT. You need some sugar.

He spoons it into her cup. Stirs it and places the cup back in her hand.

Drink it.

She looks at him.

NOOR. Was it you?

VIENNOT. What?

NOOR. They were laying in wait for me… Did you tell them I'd be there?

VIENNOT.…What?!

NOOR. You were with me… listening, when I called Gieules yesterday, when we arranged to meet…

VIENNOT. You think… I sold you out to the Gestapo? Are you…? My God!

Tell me, tell me, why did I keep you away? Huh? Why did I make you wait with me to watch, make sure, see what he really wanted… Huh? Why didn't I let you go? If it was me who set you up?

NOOR. I don't believe Gieules would… Not him. You saw how they threw him into the car, with their guns. Will they hurt him?

VIENNOT. So he couldn't betray you but I could. Fucking hell!

He gets up angrily, his chair falls back, she flinches.

NOOR. Pierre, I'm sorry. Don't –

VIENNOT. You know, you think what you want.

We'll have to tighten our watch everywhere. I have to tell / everyone.

NOOR. I'm sorry… Don't go. Please.

VIENNOT (*quietly*). You're the prize they're hunting. Poste Madeleine.

NOOR. And they can keep trying. No matter how hard they try, they won't catch me –

VIENNOT. Which makes them want you even more. You have to listen. They're closing in.

You'll have to go to the hairdressers again, okay?

She runs her hands through her hair and a clump comes out in her hand.

NOOR. No, I can't bear… all this dyeing and / cutting and –

VIENNOT. Well, you have to. And this outfit…

NOOR. What?

VIENNOT. Every Gestapo in Paris has seen you in this blue thing… How the hell you've managed to escape them all these weeks –

NOOR. Months –

VIENNOT. Fine, months. Wearing this!

And you must stop. Running around with your transmitter everywhere –

NOOR. I won't risk / someone –

VIENNOT. And the bloody notebook! Anyone could get their hands on it, look.

He grabs it off the table and she reaches for it.

NOOR. Give it! Give it to me!

VIENNOT. If a Gestapo stops you in the street and asks you / what this is?

NOOR. Stop it, that's mine! Pierre!

VIENNOT (*of the notebook*). It shouldn't even exist. It tells them everything they need to know… You have to burn it.

NOOR. Give it / to me.

VIENNOT. Okay, then I will!

NOOR. Pierre!

She lunges for him. Animal force. Gets the book out of his hands and hurts him, somehow, badly, in the process.

Just…

VIENNOT. I'm fine.

NOOR. I'm so sorry, Pierre, I didn't –

VIENNOT. I'm FINE.

A moment. He gets up. The waiter comes over to check everything's okay.

One more coffee, please.

NOOR. I should –

VIENNOT. …You need to leave your apartment. The next step is, they force someone to give your telephone / number.

NOOR. Who, who would do that?

VIENNOT. Someone desperate enough will, believe me. Then they get your address and…

You have to go back to England. To your real life.

NOOR. This is my life.

VIENNOT. Madeleine is a code name. It's not you.

She straightens out her coat. Picks up her set. Tucks her notebook away safely.

Who even is the real you?

NOOR. Thank you, Pierre. For everything. I'm very grateful –

VIENNOT. Where are you going? We'll find you a safe / house.

NOOR. Don't worry about me. This is my city.

She goes.

6. Nora Baker Part 7

Paris, VOGT*'s office in avenue Foch. 23 November 1943.*

NOOR *holds a cup of coffee, watching* VOGT *read. The remnants of dinner in front of them. After a few moments he feels her gaze and looks up.*

NOOR. …I've never seen you carrying a weapon.

VOGT. No. I don't need to.

NOOR. You know I didn't believe you, when I first arrived and you told me there would be no torture here.

He puts down his paper and looks at her.

It's funny, I've had… I don't know how many names. Across all the different parts of my life. But you… are certainly, firmly, an Ernest.

VOGT. Is that so?

NOOR. To your core.

Your eyes. So very earnest.

VOGT. Well… Nora Baker suits you well. It's… poised. And clear.

She smiles at him

That is… your real name? You weren't playing with me?

NOOR. …Almost.

VOGT. I have acquired at least some information of substance these last four weeks.

Will your French Section have told your family… what has happened to you?

NOOR (*shakes her head*). They think I'm in Africa.

VOGT. You lied to your mother?

NOOR. And my brother.

A beat.

VOGT *starts clearing away the dishes from dinner. She watches him. Then starts humming the theme from Bach's 'Fugue in G minor'.*

VOGT. Yes, that's it! That's the one!

NOOR. 'Fugue in G minor'. It came to me last night, I knew I knew it!

She hums a little more. And then he sings along with her. They enjoy finishing the phrase with a flourish, together.

Is someone fetching the things I asked for?

VOGT. Cartaud will go to your apartment tomorrow.

NOOR. Not that bastard.

VOGT. Yes, that… bastard will bring you back your – (*Reading off a bit of paper.*) face powder and more writing paper, as requested, so…

NOOR. Thank you. You're good to have organised it.

VOGT. You write most evenings in your cell, they tell me.

NOOR. Old habits die hard.

VOGT. Is it a novel you're writing?

NOOR. Just stories.

VOGT. May I read one?

NOOR. I'm sorry, Ernest, but I just can't – I won't share anything unfinished. I'm almost there with this one – as soon as I am, I promise I'll let you read it.

VOGT. I'll be very glad to.

NOOR. So it's been six weeks…

The very worst thing is… I never let my set or notebook out of my sight. I'd had an argument with someone about it and, I just… I decided to. That day. For the very first time.

And that day, that bastard, Cartaud, found his way to me.

How did you discover my address?

VOGT. That… I cannot. It is a question I never answer to a prisoner.

NOOR. Is that all I am? A prisoner?

Ernest? Who was he? That betrayed me?

Did he take money in return for my whereabouts?

He tries his best to hold her gaze.

Those honest eyes of yours. Not very good at withholding the truth, are they?

Who was it?

VOGT. I'm afraid I will not answer that.

She takes two cigarettes out of his packet, gives one to him. He lights them.

NOOR. One for me, one for you.

A moment while they smoke.

Today is… November… twenty-third?

VOGT. Twenty-fourth.

It's… past midnight. I should walk you back upstairs.

NOOR. Can't I finish my cigarette?

He comes to stand behind her. She sings a little bit from the fugue, leaning her head against him. VOGT *kisses her on the head.*

VOGT. It's late.

She finishes her cigarette and stands.

Never forget, Madeleine, I am your enemy.

Please don't forget that.

NOOR. You're not.

VOGT. Yes I am.

NOOR. You're my friend. Ernest.

VOGT. And I am also your enemy.

7. The Prize

Paris, 13 October 1943. NOOR*'s apartment on rue de la Faisanderie.* VOGT *and* CARTAUD *standing slightly awkwardly, speaking in whispers.*

VOGT. She's just gone out for a few hours, that's what –

CARTAUD. And if she doesn't come?

VOGT. You just have to wait. Quietly. She'll come.

I've got to go, give the informant the money. I'll see you back at avenue Foch.

CARTAUD. Who is he? The informant?

C'mon, Vogt… tell me.

VOGT. He is… Mademoiselle Renée Garry. The sister of Cinema.

CARTAUD. Shit!

VOGT. What?

CARTAUD. You never think a woman will turn on another.

VOGT. I checked it out. This Renée has known Madeleine since June – all her cover names, how she describes her, always dressed in blue.

CARTAUD. She informed on one of her own. Why?

VOGT. She seems to dislike her very much. And she knows how much Madeleine is worth to us.

CARTAUD *has spied the set and her notes.*

CARTAUD. Holy shit!

VOGT *goes to take a look. Using a pen, he lifts the pages of the notebook and they look through it.*

VOGT. What on earth…

CARTAUD. She's noted down her messages, all the codes. If we take her today. With this and her set –

VOGT. The radio games will be –

CARTAUD. A piece of piss.

VOGT. I have to go. Don't touch anything till she gets here. I'll lock the door and leave the key where it was.

VOGT *goes. The sound of the lock.* CARTAUD *sits in an armchair, waiting.*

Time passes. Then…

The sound of a key turning in the door. CARTAUD *springs up and hides behind the door.* NOOR *steps into her apartment and as she does, with a slam of the door,* CARTAUD *jumps her. One arm round her waist, the other over her mouth. But he needs all his force to try to contain her – he hadn't reckoned on her strength.*

NOOR. Non! Mais non! Tu ne peux pas…

It's a brutal fight – NOOR *is wild with rage, trying to get her hands up to the top of his face, his eyes;* CARTAUD *struggles with everything to keep her still.*

Tu ne peux pas, putain, sale Boche, comment oses-tu! Tu ne peux pas! Non! NON!!

Eventually she manages to grab a handful of his hair and she yanks. His grip loosens and she gets a bit of wriggle room to raise her own hands to his – she pulls his arms down and sinks her teeth into one of his wrists.

He lets out a vast scream of pain.

CARTAUD. Aaaaah!

He hasn't let go of her entirely and she takes another huge bite out of the arm still trying to restrain her. He lets her go with another huge scream and scrabbles for his gun which he raises at her.

Putain de merde!

She spits – the last bite drew blood.

NOOR. What did you just say?

His gun is trained on her and he examines the bite marks on his wrist.

CARTAUD. Filthy fucking animal!

They face one another – no one dares move.

Sit. Sit down!

She doesn't budge.

I said sit! In the fucking chair… Or I will…

NOOR. Shoot? No you won't. You want me for information, you don't want me dead.

CARTAUD. Sit down!

CARTAUD *fires a shot into the air. For a tiny moment* NOOR *is rattled by the gunshot.*

CARTAUD *looks around the room for the phone. Keeping his gun trained on her, he backs towards the telephone. She stares at him, her eyes on fire, as he dials.*

It's Cartaud, I have her, I told you I would!

No! You need to send someone, she's totally fucking crazy, I'm… I'm injured.

Send Vogt – he needs to come… take the things… her radio and books.

He hangs up.

NOOR. You sound like a Frenchman speaking German.

CARTAUD. Sit down and shut up.

NOOR. That's a very French name, Cartaud.

He approaches, pointing the gun at her face.

CARTAUD. And you have a very… dark face, Madeleine. These English are even more stupid than I thought, taking a dirty Creole to fight for them.

NOOR. At least I'm not a traitor. But… I don't need to speak to you in German, do I? Tu me comprends parfaitement en Français…

He thrusts the gun at her. She stands her ground.

Have you given it all up, your self, for a little power?

She stares him down.

CARTAUD. At least I'm not stupid – you made it so easy! We've been tracking you for weeks, in this little blue outfit. And, I mean… what kind of fucking idiot keeps a notebook like this?!

He brandishes her notebook in front of her. She reaches for it and he waves the gun right in her face.

NOOR. Donne-le! Donne-moi ça!

CARTAUD. Tttt, ttt, ttt! Calm down, calm down!

This is mine now. I got you. It's game over.

8. Nora Baker Part 8

Paris, 25 November 1943. 84 avenue Foch. The sound of air raid sirens blaring.

A GUARD *shoves* NOOR, *hands cuffed behind her back, into a room. It should look like* VOGT*'s office but not quite.*

The GUARD *locks the door from the inside. A sound of something hard and heavy making impact with a human body and an awful scream from nearby.*

NOOR. What are they doing to him?

He turns away from her.

I would like to speak with Ernest.

GUARD. Who?

NOOR. Vogt. Call him please, and ask him to come and translate for us?

GUARD. Vogt in hospital.

NOOR. No… When? I don't believe you.

GUARD. He is sick.

NOOR. Is he… okay?

An almighty thumping on the door.

GUARD. Prisoner, turn to face the wall.

The GUARD *unlocks the door.* KIEFFER *steps in wild with rage, his gun in his hand. The* GUARD *salutes him.*

Sturmbannführer.

KIEFFER*'s hand flexes around the handle of his gun as he raises it to point towards* NOOR*'s back.*

She turns her head a touch to see what is happening and on seeing the gun pointing right at her:

KIEFFER. Face the wall!

KIEFFER *fires a shot into the ground.* NOOR *screams.*

One more move, the next bullets are for you.

Now listen, I have no more time! One month we have wasted, trying to get information from you. I'm sick and tired of this bullshit, okay?

Outside is a paper, a deposition that you will not try this shit again. If you want to be alive in ten minutes' time, you sign the paper, understand?

Turn to look at me now. I said look at me.

NOOR *turns and looks straight at him.*

Do you sign the paper?

NOOR. You want me to promise I won't try to escape again?

KIEFFER. Your conspirators did it.

NOOR. Of course. Because they are cowards.

A beat.

KIEFFER. You know, I said to Vogt, first time you come here, why don't you just slap her? Give the famous Madeleinc a hard slap… One huge slap, then see. Hmm?

But all the way, he said you will cooperate, give us information. And I think he was deluded… So now we try my way.

He presses the gun right into her cheek.

NOOR. Do what you want. I will tell you nothing. You are false. I read it in your eyes.

KIEFFER *smiles.*

KIEFFER. He was soft for you, Vogt. Maybe he has a thing for the dark skin. All your tea parties and dinners… Did he get some… extra… after pouring your wine? Loosen you up first, for some fun?

Sadly he is not here. To protect you. So now you listen to me. Understand? You sign this paper, or…

NOOR. Or?

KIEFFER. We go the hard way.

Nacht und Nebel.

His hand tightens around his gun. She doesn't move.

9. Woman in Chains

Pforzheim Prison. August 1944. NOOR*'s hands and feet are manacled, in a solitary cell under maximum security. She is beaten and bruised.*

With her hands chained, she plays the imaginary piano, which is agony. Fragments of music float, not ever coming together.

A GUARD *comes in and releases her bonds, and tells her to keep quiet before going.*

The ghost of ABBA *comes to her, holding her like a child.*

NOOR. My hands… I can't get across all the notes!

ABBA. Babuli… play it again.

She plays and we hear the melody of 'Clair de Lune', faltering.

Now try singing it.

She starts singing the notes through. He joins her for the last two phrases.

Now, play it into the air.

She plays an invisible keyboard in the air, making the shapes of the chords and passing notes. He watches.

Can you hear it – (*Places a hand on her chest.*) in here?

She nods.

Good. So – what would you say is at the heart of that melody?

NOOR.…Is it the middle, duh-dah-duh daah dah, duh-dah-duh?

ABBA. It may also be the…

Silence.

…that nothing just after duh-dah-duh daah dah…

The rest. The silence. The most powerful sound. I think that's the heart, the air for you to fly.

The GUARD *comes back in. He handcuffs her again.*

GUARD. Get up. It's time to go.

10. Nacht und Nebel

11 September 1944. A train, travelling through France to Germany.

NOOR, YOLANDE, *and two other female* SOE RECRUITS, *sit looking at the passing scenery. Air washes through the carriage. They are all handcuffed. From time to time,* NOOR*'s hands play her invisible piano.*

Two Gestapo GUARDS *watch over them.*

NOOR. Where do you think we're going?

YOLANDE. Look at the leaves… those colours!

NOOR. Wanborough feels like a lifetime ago.

YOLANDE. When I got moved to Karlsruhe after the interrogations… they travelled a group of us, all girls, out of Paris. I felt so excited to be taking the train to Germany.

Crazy, when you think about it…

Where did they move you to?

NOOR. After avenue Foch, they sent me to Pforzheim. I was in solitary for… months. Someone said as I left this morning, ten months, I'm not sure.

YOLANDE. You were in solitary ten months?

NOOR. You're still beautiful. After all this time.

YOLANDE *looks to the* GUARD.

YOLANDE. Do you think he understands us?

NOOR. It takes a particular type of arrogance, mixed with a special kind of stupidity, never to want to learn another language.

NOOR *gestures towards the* GUARD. YOLANDE *sees* NOOR*'s hands playing her phantom piano.*

YOLANDE. My last week at Karlsruhe, I had this vivid dream… about my husband. I saw him so clearly. And I woke up with a pain right here… I hope…

She watches NOOR*'s hands.*

NOOR. Yes.

What did you do to make it better? The pain.

YOLANDE. I'd sew a little – that helped.

NOOR. Of course! You darning all those socks!

YOLANDE. Oh God!

NOOR. My problem is, I can't… hear clearly any more.

At Pforzheim, I would… imagine a keyboard. Into the air, or against my leg… But the chains… on my hands… I, just, I couldn't… hear it right.

YOLANDE. I'd pierce the fingertips… sometimes. Use the blood to draw.

It dries such a… strange, beautiful… like the colour of those leaves.

NOOR *gently caresses her friend's hands.*

NOOR. I'm going to ask him.

She turns to the GUARD *and speaks to him in German.*

Entschuldigung, Leutnant, wie weit ist es noch?

GUARD. Noch ein paar Stunden.

NOOR. Können Sie uns sagen, wohin Sie uns bringen?

GUARD. Irgendwo, wo es sehr grün ist. Wo viel Landwirtschaft betrieben wird.

NOOR. Danke.

She turns back to YOLANDE.

YOLANDE. Did he say a… green place?

NOOR. To do farming.

YOLANDE. Do you think he's telling the truth?

She looks around her. The countryside disappears. The noise of the train stops.

NOOR. I'm not sure any of this is the truth.

YOLANDE. No.

YOLANDE *releases the handcuffs,* MADELEINE *and* ELIANE *undo theirs and they and the* GUARDS *go.*

NOOR. So easy… to sleepwalk into an… acceptable version. Of the truth.

That was one: a tender moment… Sisterhood… with my old comrade, Yolande. Reunited after all those months… years. On a German train. Autumn leaves.

Another version: I was chucked into the back of a lorry. Alone. In scraps of clothing. Hands and feet in chains. And driven from Pforzheim to Dachau.

But I can't… I don't know which one…

Which one? Who does the truth belong to?

To war tribunals? And the confessions of German officers?

To my Bhai? And everyone else who spent years searching trying to find out what had happened to me.

Kieffer said it: Nacht und Nebel. I disappeared into night and the fog.

I can't… finish my story.

A moment of profound loss. She steps out of the space.

Can you…? I can't, I'm sorry…

VERA, BHAI *and* VIENNOT *appear.* VOGT *returns to his office in avenue Foch, alone. He is frail. He looks over the papers he had when he was with* NOOR.

VERA. No, you mustn't be. I am… sorry.

BHAI. As am I.

VERA *goes to the papers on* VOGT*'s desk. Picks up a few sheets.*

VERA. There were… a number of accounts of four women, Yolande Beekman, Madeleine Damerment, Eliane Plewman and you… arriving to Dachau on September twelfth 1944.

A number of officers testified at the tribunals that you all knelt hand in hand. At dawn, on a mound of earth. As they fired shots into the backs of your heads…

A poetic end to heroic lives.

BHAI. But the other account…

You discovered two letters.

VERA. Yes. Sent anonymously from Canada and Gibraltar. People who witnessed what happened at Dachau.

BHAI *takes a piece of paper out of his pocket.*

BHAI (*reading*). 'They did receive a group of women, three typical French and one looking more of a Creole type. The three French women were taken near the crematorium where they were partially undressed, they were in rags anyhow, and shot with pistols. They were handled very roughly.'

'The Creole…'

Forgive me, I…

He hands the sheet of paper to VIENNOT *who continues reading from where* BHAI *left off.*

VIENNOT (*reading*). 'The Creole was kept outside, chained and almost naked. She was subjected to ridicule, slapped and kicked by a man who was very fond of this type of sport. She was left all night long lying on the floor in the cell and the next day they gave her some more rough handling. Finally, in a cell they shot her with a small pistol and dead or half-dead she was carried by some other inmates and thrown into the furnace.'

VERA *takes out a folded piece of paper.*

VERA. The second letter. From Gibraltar.

'When Ruppert'… the torturer… 'got tired, and the girl'… that's you… 'was a bloody mess he told her that he would shoot her. First she had to kneel and the only word she said before Ruppert shot her from behind the head was "liberté".'

BHAI *coughs.*

BHAI. I have been trying to represent to myself what it would have been like with your nose bleeding and your eyes bleeding… I don't know.

VERA. Neither of these men were willing to declare publicly what they knew.

So how do we finish your story?

VIENNOT. You endured.

BHAI. Alone.

Nearly three hundred days.

VERA. You didn't tell them a thing.

BHAI. So many lives were saved. Because of you.

VIENNOT. And you were given medals… Maybe because someone somewhere knew they'd been culpable. A guilty… St George's Cross.

VERA. For not trying hard enough to bring you back.

BHAI. For sending you there at all… But you wanted to go. So badly, you wanted to go.

VERA. And you've been celebrated. On postage stamps, blue plaques, in history books.

BHAI. Not many history books, but some.

VIENNOT. They commend your extraordinary bravery. In the face of extreme suffering.

NOOR. Did I? Suffer… more than so many have suffered? Continue to suffer…

VOGT. You told me you'd never share an unfinished story. What about your own…?

11. Babuli 8

Suresnes, 31 December 1922. A hallway in Fazal Manzil.

In a puddle of moonlight, NOOR*'s* ABBA *cradles young* NOOR*, aged eight, who is asleep. He hums the melody of 'Clair de Lune'. She stirs.*

NOOR. Did I…?

ABBA. You've been out for another one of your walks.

NOOR. Sorry, Abba.

ABBA. Oh, / no.

NOOR. I woke you. I'm sorry –

ABBA. You have nothing to be sorry for. It's a treat to be sitting here with you. Even if it is almost midnight.

NOOR. I can still see you.

ABBA. Well… it's never absolutely dark, is it? There's always a little sliver of moon somewhere.

A clock somewhere strikes twelve.

Now, look what I happen to have, just by chance, in my pocket…

He takes out two wrapped chocolates.

NOOR. For me…?!

ABBA. Happy birthday, my little one.

She wraps her arms around him.

One for me, one for you.

NOOR *lies back down with her head in his lap. She unwraps and eats her chocolate..*

NOOR. …Abba, is it ever absolutely light?

ABBA. Hmm, I don't think our eyes could see all the light there ever is, no.

NOOR. Just pieces of it.

ABBA. Like the great elephant. You can never grasp all of him, can you?

NOOR. Not all. Just pieces. I think I would like his trunk best.

ABBA. Me too.

But the whole of him is his greatness – man yaerif nafsah yaerif rabah.

Always remember the wonderful wholeness and light of you, Noor-un-Nissa Inayat Khan.

NOOR. So… why do you call me Babuli?

He unwraps and eats his chocolate.

ABBA. Now, that is a good question. I took one look at you, tiny baby that you were, and I knew – you are your father's child.

That's what it means. That I'll always be here for you.

NOOR. What happens when you won't? Will I become someone else?

ABBA.…

It's snowing.

NOOR. Can I see?

She looks out. The world is totally white.

No! The fairies!

ABBA. Ah, that's the thing… about this world of ours. It's made of strong stuff.

See that little thing there? Poking up through the blanket of white, just there by the apricot tree… That's a flower – they call it perce-neige in the language here; we call it a snowdrop.

NOOR. Snowdrop.

ABBA. Yes. It's only small but it can break right through the cold and the dark. Such immense strength.

Just that tiny thing.

They watch the snow falling.

NOOR. It's so quiet.

The End.